The information in this b  opinion. The author has made every effort to supply accurate information in the creation and publishing of this book. The author offers no warranty or accepts any responsibility for any loss or damages of any kind that may be incurred by the reader as a result from the use of the content of this book. Reader assumes all responsibility for the use of the information in this text.

The Seed Saving Handbook:

How to Preserve Store and Start Heirloom And Organic Seeds

Urban Hillbilly

TABLE OF CONTENTS

- What are Heirloom Seeds and Why They're So Important
- Difference Between Hybrid and Open-Pollinated Seeds
- Difference Between Angiosperms and Gymnosperms
- Internal and External Factors For Seed Germination
- Best Ways To Store Your Seeds
- Growing Stages of Seeds
- How to Control Cross-Pollination
- Simple Vegetables You Can Grow At Home
- Instructions on Saving Seeds of Most Common Vegetables

What Are Heirloom Seeds and Why They're So Important

There has been much new interest in what heirloom seeds are. In the confusion, the meaning has been somewhat pulled in different directions.

Here we will discuss what are heirloom seeds and why they're so important. Traditionally an heirloom is something of value passed down from one generation to another.

It's no coincidence that an heirloom seed is a seed that has been carefully grown, saved, and passed down from one generation to another.

Often because of the considered value the particular seed has. Value could mean a seeds specific flavor, It's productivity when grown, or any other improving quality's of that plant species saved onto that seed.

Many heirloom seeds that are available now can be traced back from 100 to even 300 years ago!

For generations to have saved and preserved these for so long, the value of those seeds have been proven and considered high quality for a very long time.

Most chosen heirloom seeds are often those with the best flavor in what they produce.

Another widely saved trait is the easy of production and the ability to grow in small gardens. It is only the strongest, most adaptable, most dependable, best flavor, and most memorable varieties of seed that last the test of time. Weak, fickle, or delicate varieties become weeded out very quickly.

So now you might ask yourself Why heirloom plants?

Why not hybrids, open-pollinated, or even GMO seed?

First, lets explore the difference between hybrids and open-pollinated plants.

Open-pollination happens when the wind or insects for example pollinate the plant. Then you save the seeds that come from these plants. You can be pretty sure that the next group is going to be similar to the first.

Hybrids on the other hand are pollinated by hand to create a F1 hybrid and are very uniform. Each plant is just like the other in every way. Hybrids are often used in large scale farming. Everything grows at the same time and one plant looks just like the other.

Hybrids have been used for a very long time and are typically more expensive. These characteristics are not at all valuable to the home gardener.

Heirloom seeds are generally chosen for the best taste and healthy growth. These characteristics make it a good choice for the home gardener. But why save seed? A big reason for me is that seed is not cheap.

If you save your seed you only have to pay for it once. Once planted the plants adapt to your gardens ecosystem. If you grow a few plants each year and save the seed from the best growing plants you will unknowing have developed a strain that is resistant to pests and diseases in your garden and that is adapted to your soil and climate. Talk about a major wow factor. But I would have to say the most important reason is food security and self sufficiency.

With your own bank of plant growing knowledge and a collection of self developed seed you become less dependent on our current system that keeps food in your home.

Disasters happen, war is all around us, and not to sound like a 2012 theorist but governments sometimes fail. As far as survival actions go, saving seeds makes you seem less crazy as stockpiling weapons, gas and hoarding batteries.

A Better Understanding Hybrid and Open Pollinated Seeds

Before understanding the difference between hybrid and open pollinated seeds, it is good to know the meaning of the two phrases

Open pollination just occur naturally through the known pollination agents eg wind, insects, human beings, animals among other mechanisms.

Since there are no restrictions on how the pollen grains flow between the plants, the plants pollinated will enjoy a genetic diversity. This can cause certain variations within certain plant plantations.

This allows the plants to quickly adapt to the local climatic conditions and as long as the pollen grains are shared by plants in the same species, the offspring produced will be authentic.

Hybrid method is where the pollen grains between different species are matched through human action in order to cross breed them. Hybridization may sometimes occur naturally as a result of random cross pollination but commercially it is done intentionally to yield the desired traits.

Plant breeders cross breed compatible types of plants with the main objective being to produce a plant that has features better than those of their parents.

The concept of hybrid seems very easy to understand. Just take two plants from similar species but from different parental lineage and breeds them. The result is what is called a hybrid.

The main objective here is to look for two plants, the best in the parental line, and cross them to make a strong combination. This seems to be a great idea.

However, although the offspring will be bigger, more colorful and grows faster, the result can disappoint you. The fruit or vegetable will not have adequate minerals and vitamins.

It may also lack original flavor and may also be much harder to grow because of the time, energy, and maintenance involved. Hybrid plants require much more water, more fertilizers, and more chemicals; this is the reason why they don't yield for a long time.

Open pollinated seeds are produced naturally and do not require any human interaction. Open pollinated seeds keep on changing from time to time, adapt to the environment and are not difficult to grow. Plants grown from the open pollinated seed have much resistance to fungus and pests.

They also do not require so much fertilizer and can even thrive with organic fertilizers. Since they are so dynamic and are able to adapt to changing conditions, they may not require so much water. The main advantage of using cross pollinated seeds is that they will yield continuously after each year and you can save the seeds.

Hybrid seeds are not so expensive. On the other hand, open pollinated seeds are quite expensive. However it can be wise to buy open pollinated price and enjoy their advantages.

With open pollinated seeds, you only need to make the initial purchase and from there you can reserve some of their harvest and plant it again.

You can repeat this cycle time and again and you will still get a good harvest. It is good to spend money in a high quality product than purchase low quality products at a low cost.

What's the Difference Between Angiosperms and Gymnosperms?

Seed-bearing plants are divided into two broad categories - Angiosperms and Gymnosperms. On a general level, they are distinguished on the basis of their ability to bear flowers and fruit.

However, each group has distinct characteristics which form the basis of their classification. The article is an in-depth on the differences between angiosperms and gymnosperms.

The Difference in Anatomy

The main point of difference between angiosperms and gymnosperms lies in the structure of their seeds. The word Gymnosperm has the Greek word "gymnosperms" as its root. This is also known as "Naked Seed". It is an apt name because the seed does not have an outer, protective covering. On the contrary, the seeds of angiosperms are enclosed within structures that later develop into fruits. Conifers are the most well-known gymnosperms.

There are also differences in the structure of the leaves. Typically, the leaves of an angiosperm are flat as compared to the needle-like or scale-like appearance of the leaves of gymnosperms.

The Presence/Absence of Fruits and Flowers

Gymnosperms do not bear any flowers and fruit. Their seeds are contained in cones or on the scales of leaves. The cones are unisexual.

They do not disperse their seeds in fruit, but rely on animals and the wind to carry their seeds to other locations. Angiosperms are flowering plants. Flowers can either be unisexual or bisexual. They disperse their seeds in fruit. Since the fruit is nothing but a ripened plant ovary, animals and birds become the main carriers of seeds when they eat and excrete it.

Mode of Reproduction/Fertilization

Angiosperms and gymnosperms also differ in the manner in which they reproduce.

A gymnosperm produces male and female cones. The males tend to be smaller than females. Also, female cones take longer to mature and hence, retain a green color rather than turning brown immediately.

The male cones produced sperms contained in pollen grains while the female ones produces eggs contained in ovules. In addition to the eggs, the female cones also produce a sticky resin to attract pollens when the winds disperse them. Fertilization occurs inside the female cone. It gradually grows in size, the scales separates and the seeds drop out.

The flower in an angiosperm houses the male anatomy, the female anatomy and the sterile structures. The stamen produces and releases sperm-containing pollen grains.

During pollination, the stigma attracts pollen grains. When pollination occurs, the sperm cell is transferred to the ovule in the ovary via a pollen tube. Fertilization occurs when the sperm cell unites with the egg in the ovule.

Endosperm Tissue

The endosperm tissue in gymnosperms is a haploid tissue as it is formed before fertilization. It is a triploid tissue in angiosperms as it is the result of double fertilization and triple fusion.

Variation

Although it is not a very often noted and citied difference between angiosperms and gymnosperms, the former is more varied than the latter. It is to say that angiosperms can be large trees, shrubs or herbs. However, gymnosperms are typically woody trees namely Pine, Fir, Cypress, Redwood, Juniper, Spruce and Cycads. Gymnosperms are hardwood varieties while angiosperms are softwood varieties.

Life Cycle

Most angiosperms are seasonal plants. As such, they are non-perennial plants. Gymnosperms are evergreen plants; they do not wither and die seasonally. They grow and flourish throughout the year.

Who came first?

Although not a major difference between angiosperms and gymnosperms, it is worth noting who came first. Gymnosperms existed several millions years before angiosperms sprouted on the surface of the earth.

However today, angiosperms are considered the most dominant form of vegetation. It is also very widely distributed comprising of a wide range of plants.

Internal and External Factors For Seed Germination

Seed germination is the process that turns a mature seed into a plant. Each seed contain an embryo and most have a food supply inside a seed coat.

Occasionally a seed will not have an embryo and will never germinate. Most seeds go through a period of dormancy where the seed will not grow.

This is so the seed can be transported to a different area before it germinates. There are two types of dormancy. The first is seed coat dormancy which delays germination until the seed coat is worn away, removed from fruit, ingested by an animal, broken or even heated in fire.

The second is embryo dormancy where the genetics of the plant determine ideal conditions for germination

External Factors

Seeds will need proper temperature, water, oxygen, and light in order to germinate.

- **Water**

A mature seed is very dry. In order for cell metabolism to resume, the seed will need to take in a lot of water relative to the weight of the seed itself.

This water causes the inside of the seed to swell helping the seed coat to break open. When the seed takes in water it also produces enzymes that break down the stored food in the seed so the embryo can use it to grow.

Once the seedling emerges from the seed and starts growing roots and leaves the stored food is usually used up. By this time the plant is able to create its own energy by the process of photosynthesis and will need a continuous supply of water, nutrients and light to continue to grow.

Temperature - Temperature affects metabolism and growth rates of seeds and seedlings. Each type of seed has a range of temperatures at which it will germinate. Most seeds will germinate at room temperature in a centrally heated house.

Some need temperatures just above or even below freezing while others need much warmer temperatures. For example, peas can sprout in the ground at temperatures as low as 40 degrees F. Pumpkins on the other hand need soil temperatures of 65 degrees F before they can germinate.

Temperature also affects the dormancy of seeds. Some seeds require a period of cold before they will sprout. Some require several shifts of temperature to break dormancy. Some even need the heat of a forest fire to crack open their seed coat.

- **Oxygen**

Germinating seeds require oxygen for the energy needed to metabolize the stored food supply. Oxygen is found in the pore spaces in soil as well as in the air.

If the soil is waterlogged the seed will not get enough oxygen and will be oxygen starved. Some plants have seed coats that do not allow oxygen to pass until the seed coat is worn down or damaged. Seeds of this type have a physical dormancy.

- **Light**

Light or lack of light does not affect all seeds. Some seeds have to have sunlight to grow. For example, common crabgrass seeds need sunlight to sprout. This condition is common in forest plants as well where they need a break in the forest canopy in order to grow.

Best Ways To Store Your Seeds

Nothing can beat the effectiveness and health benefits of home grown organic and fresh vegetables such as tomatoes, peas, carrots, spinach, Swiss chard, lettuce, cabbage, kale, cucumbers, squash, beets, pumpkins and many more to name of.

In order to grow these most common vegetables you need to save their respective seeds.

In this article, we are going to reveal very simple and probably the best ways to store your seeds of given home grown veggies.

Things you should remember while storing vegetables seeds

Normally veggies seeds can be stored for one whole year at room temperature without losing their power to germinate significantly. If you are willing to store these seeds for 10 years or so, then you need to dry seeds at 100 degrees (F) for six hours. Generally less than 8 % moisture is recommended for long shelf life of vegetable seeds.

- Do not expose your seeds to direct sunlight or microwave as this will ruin them to a great extent. Let the seeds dry in a shade.

You can make the seeds drying process quick by using a conventional oven at 500 F, but the door of the oven should be kept open during the whole process of drying.

Best Tips For Storing Home Grown Vegetables Seeds

Container in which you are about the store any seeds of veggies should be completely dry.

Refrigerator is the best place to store the seeds, so try to store seeds inside your refrigerator.

- Do not ever try to freeze your seeds as this will ruin the seeds completely.
- You can also use silica gel to remove extra moisture inside the container. But replace silica gel pallets every six months.
- Keep or store seeds in the plastic airtight bags (Zip-lock bags) and glass containers with tight lids.
- Putting dates on the container will help you distinguish between old and new stored seeds.
- Remove container from refrigerator and let it stay like for an hour or so until container attains the room temperature. Now you can plant seed without any problems whatsoever.

Most home grown vegetables seeds can be saved or stored in almost similar manner, but you should keep an eye on their respective temperature ranges and time as well.

Dry milk powder wrapped into tissue paper layers can also be used to keep the seeds dry or moisture free. Spread vegetable seeds on a dry newspaper to air dry them for approximately one whole week. If you are trying to air dry different seeds simultaneously, then it's better for you to put their names or labels on the newspapers to avoid mixing them up.

Some seeds have strong germination rate compared with other seeds. So it is essential to plant or consume those seeds quickly that have low germination rate.

If you are willing to save your own vegetable seeds, then always plant Open Pollinated (OP) varieties. On the other hand, hybrid seeds varieties won't excel as much as Open Pollinated varieties.

In conclusion, we can say that almost any vegetable seeds can be stored by completely following the above mentioned tips or techniques. These given best ways to store your seeds can really help you save your time and money at later stages.

Growing Stages of Seeds

Seed is a unit of reproduction of plant and a new plant is formed through a seed. In the absence of a right seed, the plant will not be able to reproduce and eventually that specie will go extinct.

Life-cycle of any plant could be split into various levels and seed germination is the first level in the growth of any plant. A seed is the life of a plant in an embryonic condition.

The moment it gets favorable atmosphere, the seed starts to grow. During the growth, all seeds demand enough oxygen, water, and right temperature. A few seeds may need adequate lighting too.

Some could germinate nicely in the presence of light, while some may require darkness to begin germination. Water is essential for initiation and for maintaining the pace of process. Right soil temperature is also essential for correct germination. The optimum soil temperature for each seed varies.

The seeds of angiosperms can be divided into two categories, dicotyledons or dicots and monocotyledons or monocots and the stages of seed growth differ in both.

There are generally three stages of seed germination. In the beginning, seed lies dormant into the soil. The seed rests in the soil for a time being and as soon as the required conditions to begin the growth are met, the seed starts the process. The process begins from hydrating the seed and the seed completely grows when the cotyledons emerge out.

Stage 1: Hydration and Metabolism

The seed absorbs water from the damp soil. This process is called 'imbibitions'. Absorption of water softens the coat of the seed and initiates metabolism process. The water triggers a chain of chemical reaction by releasing an enzyme. The enzymes get activated, and cellular respiration speeds up. Because of the respiration the starch present inside the seed is transformed into sugar.

Stage 2 : Nourishment

At the second stage, seed breaks the food down. Lipids and carbohydrates in the seed breaks down into sucrose, and this sucrose is and broken down proteins are trans located to a location in the seed where they can be used for energy for growing plant. Soon, the embryo gets all the nourishment and increases in size.

Stage 3 : Cell division and Growth

At this stage, the plant becomes the true autotroph. During this stage, the metabolism continues and the cells of the embryo continue to clone. Soon, the embryo becomes too large for the seed's coating to contain it. The coating finally ruptures and the plant begins to emerge out. First, slight portion of the root bulb comes out of the seed and starts growing in the downward direction.

The root helps in anchoring the seed in place during the growing stages of seeds. Also, it allows the embryo to absorb minerals from the soil. Later, the seeding reaches up in the air to begin the process of photosynthesis.

After the seeds germinate entirely, the roots hold the plant into the soil, giving the sprouted seed water and minerals from it and the shoot grows upward, manufacturing food for the plant through photosynthesis.

A Guide to Controlling Cross-Pollination

One of the best things about open-pollinated vegetables is their ability to produce pure seeds. This means that the seeds gotten from open-pollinated plants will produce exact replicas of the parent plant once they have been planted.

Cross pollination is likely to cause problems for gardeners wishing to save the seeds of their vegetables from year to year. Unintended cross pollination can alter the traits that a gardener wants to keep in the vegetable he/she is growing. Below is a look at how to control cross-pollination.

There are several ways of preventing vegetables from cross-pollinating. One of them is mechanical isolation or physical barriers like caging or bagging.

Insect pollinated vegetables can be protected from cross-pollination by application of the bagging technique. It involves covering the female flower with a bag in a way that pollinators cannot get into it.

The flower should be covered with a light material bag such as muslin, or with a paper. Plastic bags should not be used to for bagging flower heads since the flower can get slimy or fry in the sun. Such flowers would then be totally unsuitable for seed production.

In the case of self-pollinating vegetables, the blossoms should be covered with a bag as soon as they appear. The bag should be fastened to the stem in a way that it does not hurt the plant. A cotton ball can be used under the bag edge and then tied off using a twist-tie or thick thread.

Placing a cotton ball is such a position will prevent insects from reaching the flower. Once it is observed that the fruits are forming, the bag can be taken off without any further worries. Physical barrier techniques like bagging do not need much time to perfect.

Another method of preventing cross-pollination is by growing only one variety of a vegetable species in the garden. It is unlikely that cross pollination will take place if only a single variety of a plant species is present.

However, there is a very slight chance that pollen could be carried into the vegetables by a stray pollinating insect. For gardeners wishing to grow several varieties, they need to determine if the vegetable they plan to grow is either self, insect or wind pollinated. Accidental cross pollination is unlikely to happen in self-pollinated vegetables, although it is still quite possible. Chances of cross pollination in such vegetables can be eliminated by planting various varieties of the same species at least ten feet apart.

In the case of insect or wind pollinated vegetables, they need pollination from flowers on other vegetables of either different or the same varieties in order to produce healthy seeds. Cross pollination can be prevented by planting different varieties at least 100 yards or more.

However, the distance required for isolation of wind-pollinated plants will vary depending on the existing conditions. Wind strength and patterns, existence of windbreaks, and many other conditions all have an effect. For instance, wind-pollinated vegetables grown in low-wind, wooden areas will require much less distance when compared to those planted in open and vast windy areas.

Simple Vegetables You Can Grow at Home

We all know how delicious some vegetables you buy at a farmer's market are as opposed to vegetables you buy in a supermarket. Wouldn't it be nice if you could grow some of those at home? Of course in the process you would also save some money, which might prove to be a nice bonus as well.

Here's a list of some of the most common vegetables and how you might save their seeds.

- **Tomatoes:**

Tomatoes are a bit tricky, so a little fermentation helps. Cut the tomato in half, scoop out the seeds and the goo surrounding them and then add some water. Leave to ferment for 3 to 5 days, if a moldy film appears on top that's fine. After fermentation is done, add some more water and stir. Good seeds sink, so pour out water and goo, then leave seeds to dry on a paper plate. When thoroughly dried, place in an airtight container.

- **Potatoes:**

Whole potatoes are kept as seeds, a well ventilated, dark, and cool storage area is best. Ideal temperatures are just above freezing, between one and four degrees Celsius.

- **Lettuce:**

You'll need to let your lettuce bloom to get seeds. The flowers are yellow, similar to dandelions. Like dandelions they turn into fluffy balls. When the flower heads look dry it's time to harvest. Clean the chaff and store in a cool and dry place.

- **Spinach/Swiss Chard:**

Identify female plants, as only they will give you seeds. Once the plants turn yellow, pull them up and hang in a dark dry place. After a few weeks the seeds will turn brown and dry. Always store in a dark and cool place.

- **Cabbage/Kale/Collards:**

After leaving plants to flower, they will produce pods. Allow pods to dry to a light brown color before you pick them and open them. Be careful not to pick green pods, as these will rarely give you germinating seed.

- **Cucumbers:**

Cucumbers grown for seeds should be left in the garden at least 5 weeks after you'd normally pick them for eating. Scrape seeds and the surrounding goo in a container; add water and leave to ferment for a few days. Good seeds will sink to the bottom, so pour out water and goo, then leave to dry on a paper plate.

- **Squash and Pumpkins:**

Leave squash on vines until outer shell hardens, then leave another 3 - 4 weeks after harvesting to allow seeds to further ripen. Cut squash and scoop out the seeds, washing them then leaving to dry.

- **Beans:**

Leave on vines for about six weeks after eating stage, pods should be dry and brown. Open pods and clean chaff. Store in a cool and dry place.

- **Peas:**

Leave pods on vines for about four weeks after eating stage, pods should turn dry and brown. Open pods and clean chaff. And Store in a cool and dry place.

- **Carrots:**

Leaving carrots to flower will produce a round, flat group of flowers called umbel. Pick umbels as they dry brown, leave to mature in a cool and dark place for further two to three weeks. Get seeds by rubbing umbels between your hands, then winnow and clean.

- **Beets:**

Cut the flower just above the root, as it turns brown. Remember to store in cool, dry place allowing seeds to mature. Mature seeds can be easily picked by hand.

- **Radishes:**

Harvest seedpods when they have turned dry and brown. Open pods by hand and clean any chaff.

Seed Saving

Seed saving is also known as brown bagging and it is the technique used to save the seed and other important reproductive material from the vegetables plants. This is used for the further reproduction of plants, grains and herbs. This is also known as traditional way of farming and gardening.

- **Tomato**

It is easy to save the seeds for the tomato in your own garden. The process of seed saving is a part of the process of fermentation. Choose some of the healthiest tomatoes from the plants and slice it. Now, scoop out all the inner part from the tomato in a clean container.

Then put a plastic wrap over it and provide a small hole in this plastic wrap. Put the whole container to a warm place and give time to dry up. After some days remove the plastic wrap, stir the solution and then again put the plastic wrap with a hole. After few days remove the plastic wrap and separate the seeds from the other material. Now, put the seeds in a clean plate and give time for dry up thoroughly. Your seeds are ready and you can use them for the gardening.

- **Potato**

Saving the seeds for potato is little risky because of the disease. Potato is very prior to the disease in the very first generation. So look for that clearly and after selecting the right potatoes cut off the tops off completely. There will be a gentle bush around the potato and confirm the tubers also. Now, set them the potatoes under the cover in the sunlight for three to four days. This may turn up green and it is a good sign. Then remove the any part of soil carefully and then store the potato in frost free place.

- **Lettuce**

Lettuce plants have yellow colored flowers which contains the dandelions. When the temperature is too hot then the leaves of the plant become bitter and it makes sure that it is the right time for blooming. In the yellow flowers there are dandelions which are ready to provide seeds, isolate the pan and after 12-24 days you can enjoy the seedlings of lettuce.

- **Spinach**

It is very easy to save seeds for spinach. Just make sure that there is no wind so that there is no pollination. When the plant turns yellow and after some days of drying then the color of seeds turns brown and it is easy to save the seeds.

- **Cabbage**

These provide the problems of cross pollination and thus it is required to isolate completely. Just don't permit them to flowered and save the seeds.

- **Cucumber**

The process is same as for tomatoes. First let the cucumber ripen thoroughly and when dried up then put the inner mass in a jar of

water. Make the time for fermentation to five days and then clear the seeds and dry them thoroughly.

- **Beans**

Give time to bean for being fully mature on the vine. Give them proper time for the drying up and they turn into little brown. After them remove the pods and cover over the beans and seeds are ready.

- **Carrot and Beets**

These are biennial and flowered in the second year. These can cross pollinate. These produce a lot of seeds in the second year. It is required to bag the blooms for both carrot and beets. Save the seeds and label them and store them.

If you have truly found value in my publications please take a minute and rate my books, I'd be eternally grateful if you left a review on Amazon. As an independent author I rely on reviews for my livelihood and it gives me great pleasure to see my work is appreciated.

Made in the USA
Columbia, SC
26 September 2021